POSTCARD HISTORY SERIES

Yosemite
National Park

IN VINTAGE POSTCARDS

POSTCARD HISTORY SERIES

Yosemite National Park

IN VINTAGE POSTCARDS

Tammy Lau and Linda Sitterding

ARCADIA
PUBLISHING

Copyright © 2000 by California State University, Fresno and Fresno County Library
ISBN 978-0-7385-0884-9

Published by Arcadia Publishing
Charleston, South Carolina

Printed in the United States of America

Library of Congress Catalog Card Number: 00-105509

For all general information contact Arcadia Publishing at:
Telephone 773-549-7002
Fax 773-549-7190
E-mail sales@arcadiapublishing.com
For customer service and orders:
Toll-Free 1-888-313-2665

Visit us on the Internet at www.arcadiapublishing.com

CONTENTS

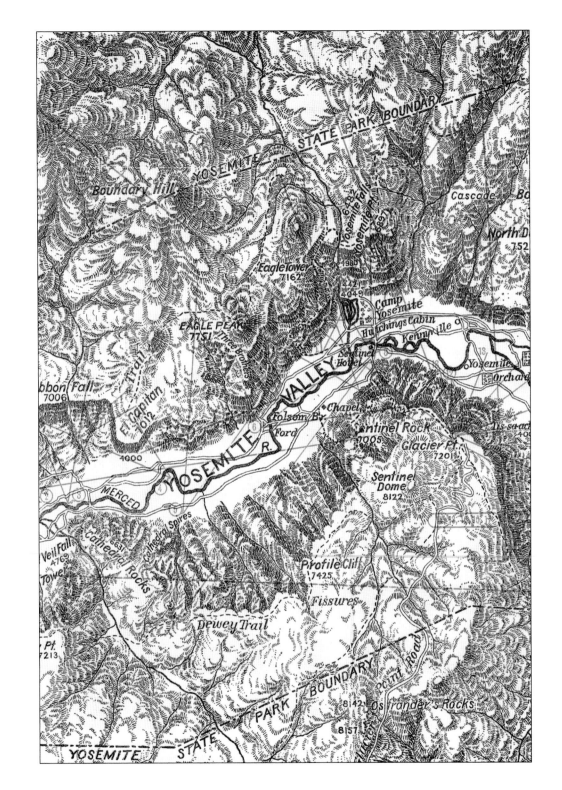

INTRODUCTION

Yosemite Valley and its environs have been known to the Native Americans of the area—the Paiutes and later the Sierra Miwoks—for thousands of years. A group of the Miwoks who lived in and around Yosemite called the valley Ahwahnee, meaning "place of the gaping mouth." They called themselves the Ahwahneechees, people of the Ahwahnee. It wasn't until 1833 that the first non-Indians encountered Yosemite. That year, an exploratory expedition comprised of 60 hunters and trappers led by Joseph R. Walker crossed the rugged Sierra Nevada into Yosemite Valley. There they encountered the natural splendors of the valley and began to make them known to the world.

The discovery of gold in California in 1848, and the infamous Gold Rush that ensued, brought thousands of eager prospectors to the area, who, armed with guns and the overweening conviction that they were superior to the Native Americans, proceeded to clash with the original inhabitants, believing they had every right to take over their land and push them out. Skirmishes and violence erupted, and in 1851, California governor John McDougal empowered a volunteer militia, the Mariposa Battalion, to subdue or eliminate the Native Americans who stood in their way. Chief Tenaya's tribe surrendered to the Battalion, but by favorable happenstance, many of the original names for features in the valley were retained and recorded by Dr. Lafayette Bunnell, a private with the Battalion. It was Bunnell who named the valley "Yosemite," because as he understood it, that was the name of Chief Tenaya's tribe.

Discovery of the giant sequoia trees in 1852, and the resultant publicity about the trees and the natural beauty of the area, prompted the effort to have Yosemite Valley and the Mariposa Grove of Big Trees designated as a public preserve, an unprecedented move at the time. The Yosemite Grant bill, which made provisions for the "preservation of the Yosemite Valley and the Big Tree Grove...for the benefit of mankind," was passed by the U.S. Congress in 1864. This was the beginning of Yosemite's future as a national park.

Much has changed over the years in the park as well as in our collective attitude towards conservation and preservation. In the late 1800s, nature was viewed as something to be tamed and made "useful." That idea was part of the American notion of "Manifest Destiny." Even within the national parks, policies on use often overrode concern for the natural environment. It has only been relatively recently that the public has embraced the idea of leaving nature the way it is and not trying to interfere with the natural order. Park management, in turn, continues to struggle with balancing the competing demands of responsible stewardship and managing use. Millions of tourists visit Yosemite each year, and the demands for park services often conflict with preservation concerns. Still, the Yosemite of today exists due to the foresight of the few, for the enjoyment of the many.

The photographic image, picture postcards, and Yosemite National Park have all evolved and matured together. In the 1870s and 1880s, as photographs became more common, the first postcards were produced in Germany. Yosemite was one of the popular sites portrayed in innumerable ways. The first postcards were used as advertisements for businesses, a practice that continued into the 1940s. Early postcards from 1901 to 1907 provided no space for a personal message, except sometimes in a little white area on the front of the card. From 1907 on, however, the familiar divided back became common, with space on the right for the recipient's address and a personal message on the left. Most of the postcards shown in this book date from the 1900s to the 1920s, with some from the 1940s. During most of this period, the postal rate to send a postcard domestically was 1¢.

The antique and curious stereoview was once as common in the Victorian and Edwardian parlor as the television is in the contemporary American living room. These rectangular cards with double photographic images side by side and detailed descriptions on the back were sold door-to-door and by subscription. Throughout the United States, whole neighborhoods and towns were canvassed, and sales strategies were plotted by summertime college students. Stereoviews were touted and marketed as entertainment and educational tools. Schools and libraries purchased stereoviews in sets numbering in the hundreds.

The stereoview offered the mystery, entertainment, and lure of foreign travel without the danger, discomfort, and expense. It was the perfect armchair traveler's vehicle. Anyone could use the viewer (called a stereoscope) and instantly see the wonders of the Nile, visit Venice, and stand at Stonehenge—all in 3-D. The stereoview, probably more than anything else before radio and television, broke down the insularity of the United States and brought its citizens into the community of the world. An elderly man in Iowa along with a young woman in Washington could both visit Siam, see the sights, observe the culture, and put the viewer down with a better understanding of a foreign place and its people.

In the United States, there were many companies and photographers that produced stereoviews from the 1860s through the 1930s. Some cards were one of a kind, produced as souvenirs of travel or mementos of a loved one, but most were duplicated many thousand times over. Keystone, Griffith and Griffith, H.C. White, and Underwood and Underwood were four companies whose total production numbers ran into the millions. The heyday of the stereoview was probably between 1880 and 1915, although stereoviews were published many years prior to 1880 and for many years after 1915.

All of the original stereoviews and postcards reproduced in this book are housed in the California History Room in the main branch of the Fresno County Library, or in the Sanoian Special Collections Library at the Madden Library of California State University, Fresno. The stereoviews are in black and white, but most of the actual postcards are in color. The authors have made every attempt to be accurate, verifying facts from different sources, but in many cases, the spellings and dimensions vary from source to source. Older books in particular have been problematic in this way. In such cases, more modern interpretations have been used. We hope you enjoy this "tour" of Yosemite's past. It's been a bumpy road, but one heck of a ride.

One

YOSEMITE IN YOUR PARLOR

Although never mailed like postcards, stereographs served the same promotional purposes that postcards did. Both featured photographic images that played a pivotal role in the genesis of Yosemite Park. Carleton E. Watkins lovingly photographed Yosemite Valley in the early 1860s. His images were printed on oversized or mammoth prints and sent to Congress. Watkins's art exposed members of Congress to the wonders of Yosemite Valley, which may have done more to insure the preservation of Yosemite than any other factor. Watkins also produced a set of stereoviews that were unrivaled for their artistry and technical grace. Everyone was eager to "see" this stupendous work of nature. Yosemite's location in the middle of California, with some of the toughest terrain in the United States between the average tourist and the granite wonders, made travel to the park difficult. The photographic image was the compromise; people could tour the wonders of Yosemite from the comfort of their own homes. Moreover, they could see these sights in three-dimensional glory.

Other photographers quickly jumped on the Yosemite bandwagon and produced series of stereoviews of Yosemite Valley. The images in this book were selected from the Underwood and Underwood publication, *Yosemite Valley: Through the Stereoscope* (1902). The Fresno County Library has allowed access to this stereograph collection in order to provide you with an old-fashioned parlor tour of the park and a peek into the past. The captions in this chapter try to capture the flavor of the flowery, hyperbolic descriptions on the back of each stereoview card. The map that came with the *Stereoscope* book is correlated to different views described in the book (see p. 6 for a reproduction of the map).

From Inspiration Point. Inspiration Point provides an appropriate introduction to the unsurpassed beauties of the park. The first white explorers came upon this awesome wilderness in 1851. The names of the cliffs, creeks, and cascades remind visitors of the old Indian legends and traditions learned from the peoples who used to roam these mountainsides.

Yosemite lies about 170 miles from San Francisco. The valley extends east and west for almost 6 miles across the general line of the Sierras. The waterfall pouring over Cathedral Rocks at the right is 40 feet wide. It plunges 900 feet to break into spray on the rocks below.

El Capitan with Half Dome in the Distance. The most striking formation in the valley is El Capitan. From its situation on the valley floor, it rises 3,300 feet. The south and west sides join at almost right angles to present a perpendicular granite face. To the lower right sits Half Dome (4,972 feet), which vies with El Capitan for the honor of the most remarkable feature in Yosemite Valley.

Ribbon Fall Looking North from the Valley. Ribbon Fall, also known as "The Virgin's Tears," drops 1,500 feet from the skyline. After the first fall strikes, it passes through innumerable cascades to a shorter leap, hidden by the trees from this point of view, and passes on to the Merced (Spanish for "mercy") River, 2,600 feet below from the granite rim. The verdant timber stand climbing the talus, bears witness to John Muir's statement that he found flowers in bloom throughout the year, even in midwinter.

El Capitan, a Solid Granite Mountain. El Capitan ("the captain") rises five-eighths of a mile above the Merced River, which mirrors its image to double the impact of this great granite bulk. The waters of the river come from snowmelt in the Sierras. The river is fed all along its route by creeks that run off the edge of the overlooking cliffs to join with the Merced hurrying to the Pacific over 170 miles away.

The Three Brothers (Eagle Peak in Center). From the south bank of the Merced River, the Three Brothers appear about a mile further up the valley than El Capitan. According to tradition, the name was given to the peaks when the valley was discovered in 1851. Several Indians were captured on the rocky talus at the foot, three of them being sons of the old Yosemite Chief Tenaya. The old Indian name meant "heads of frogs ready to leap." The highest of the three is Eagle Peak, 3,830 feet high. The view from its summit is one of the finest in the park.

North Dome, Half Dome, and Cloud's Rest. North Dome (7,525 feet) towers over the Royal Arches, ahead 3.5 miles. The Arches and North Dome are part of the same mountain and illustrate two methods of granite lamination. Notice that the layers of granite are tilted into distinct arches. Cloud's Rest, at 10,000 feet above sea level, lies 8 miles distant in the center. In the distance, right from center, Half Dome rises. The dark slope on the right leads up to Glacier Point and Glacier Dome.

Mirror View of the Majestic Cathedral Rocks—Looking West, Southwest. After the rush of Bridalveil and Yosemite Falls, here is the extreme contrast of water in repose. The image was taken in the morning when the rising sun shines full on Cathedral Rocks, whose spires cleave the sky, 2,660 feet above.

Amidst Yosemite's Charms—the Sentinel Hotel. The plain but comfortable Sentinel Hotel was the only hotel in the valley. The world-famous Ahwahnee Hotel now accommodates park visitors. Additional quarters could be found at Camp Yosemite, a tent settlement near the falls, or at Camp Curry, 2 miles up the valley beneath Glacier Point. The Upper Yosemite Fall dwarfs the hotel on its descent from the cliff in a tremendous leap of 1,500 feet.

Yosemite Point and Wind-sprayed Yosemite Falls. The first fall is a clear descent of 1,600 feet. The air currents swirl and toss the waters into a spray so fine that it appears to be dense steam. When the aerated waters reach 1,500 feet from the lip, they strike a projecting ledge and scatter in a thousand cascades down a rugged descent of 626 feet over granite debris. The struggling streams unite for a final plunge in one single sheet down the grim rock where they strike the true talus and find their rest in the Merced River.

13

The Valley, Half Dome, Nevada Fall, Cap of Liberty, and Imposing Sierras from Eagle Peak. From the summit of Eagle Peak at 7,750 feet above the sea, the scene differs dramatically from the valley. Below lies part of the valley and Half Dome. About midway to the right is the thin silver glint of the upper portion of Nevada Fall. The vast solitudes of the high Sierras lie beyond.

Yosemite Falls, from Glacier Point Trail. This viewpoint is from the trail up to Glacier Point at an open space about 1,000 feet above the valley. The vista of Yosemite Falls' 2,500-foot drop stands unobstructed. The Upper Fall leaps 1,500 feet, then the Middle Fall, made up of cascades dashing 400 feet more, and finally the Lower Fall drops 600 feet. There are two lateral ridges on the cliff that force the waters into three falls. The ridges have been worn by erosion, and it is likely that in ages past, the Yosemite fell in a single plunge of 2,600 feet. The riders who have stopped here have been on the trail for one hour, and it will take them two more hours to reach the top. The girl is riding astride as all women should on these trails.

Looking Straight Up the Face of Glacier Point. The imposing face of Glacier Point, seen from the bottom of the cliff looking upward, provides high contrast for the next image. The more common view of Glacier Point is seen looking down this sheer face from the Overhanging Rocks above.

Looking Down from Overhanging Rocks, Glacier Point into the Valley Below. From this height, the valley floor lies more than a half mile off. One can only marvel at the forces of nature that carved this terrain.

Nearly a Mile Straight Down and Only a Step—Yosemite from Glacier Point. To the left is the overhanging rock. One false step, and there is nothing but a mile of space below. The view is level with Yosemite Falls. Several miles away down the valley, Half Dome and Cloud's Rest ornament the skyline.

Overlooking Nature's Grandest Scenery...Yosemite Valley. This is the second projecting rock at Glacier Point. It was to the left in the preceding image. It appears that with a good jump, one could land on the bald pate of the Half Dome, more than 2.5 miles off. It is really 1,700 feet higher than the projecting rock, although it appears to be below Glacier Point.

From Glacier Point up Tenaya Canyon, over Mirror Lake, Half Dome, and Cloud's Rest. This view is straight up the valley of the Tenaya. Down this gorge, at the dawn of the geological history of the park, flowed a portion of the great Tuolumne glacier, which came westward and swept the floor of the Tenaya Valley clean.

Nevada and Vernal Falls, and Cap of Liberty—from Glacier Point to Mt. Clark. This image faces southeast, exactly 180 degrees in the opposite direction of the images on page 16, directly along the valley of the Merced River. Those are the Nevada and Vernal Falls.

Amid the Majestic Heights and Chasms of Wonderful Yosemite Valley—from the Trail to North and Basket Domes. The altitude of this perspective is about 7,000 feet, looking across the valley straight over to North Dome, which is 7,525 feet high. It is an awesome scene in this land of immense distances. The great Yosemite chasm makes the most impressive showing of granite rock. After geologic convulsions pulled the valley floor down and piled the mountains higher, slow-moving glaciers ground off the earlier mountain contours into new shapes. The scars of glacial travel are visible on the cliffs.

On the Brink of a Fearful Chasm—from Glacier Canyon to Half Dome. This is the beginning of the overhanging granite slab. Immediately below is a huge expanse of space. A stone dislodged here would find no rest for 2,000 feet. To the right is one of the farthest outlying spurs of Mt. Starr King.

Climbing up the Steep Zig Zag Trail at the Eastern End of the Valley. The zig zag trails have made the park accessible to horseback parties and hikers. They are used with comfort by both sexes. Without them, travel would be limited to only the hardiest individual willing to scramble over this rocky terrain.

Nevada Falls and Cap of Liberty. This view is exactly opposite the Cap of Liberty, in old times called Mt. Broderick, which towers 1,800 feet above the falls.

Mirror Lake, Looking Northeast to Mt. Watkins. Tiny Mirror Lake reflects the grandeur of the park on its placid waters. Its reflective power is surrounded by scenery found nowhere else in the world. On its clear face lies the mighty bulk of North Dome, 5,000 feet high. Above that is Mt. Watkins, more than 6,000 feet above the mirroring waters; Half Dome and Cloud's Rest cast their images into the lake at sunrise. At sunset, Glacier Point, 2 miles due southwest, fills shores of that magic pool.

From Cloud's Rest over Lake Tenaya to the Distant Matterhorn. At 10,000 feet above sea level, this is a different world of wide horizons and bleak aspects. To the right is the Matterhorn looming 12,000 feet in altitude. Mt. Dana and Mt. Warren raise their mightier bulks, and Mt. Gibbs and Mono Pass lead onward to the lake with the same name.

From Cloud's Rest over Little Yosemite Valley to Mt. Clark. Here the southern outlook is more verdant. The hills are tree-clad, and the valleys are more of a refuge from harsh weather. Mt. Clark raises its head into the heavens, and the everlasting hills proclaim their glory and might.

Vernal and Nevada Fall. The great cliff, over 7,000 feet in altitude above the Merced River, provides the backdrop for Vernal and Nevada Fall. From the Little Yosemite Valley, the river drops 2,000 feet in 2 miles to the main valley. The upper cataract is Nevada Fall, lying to the right of the Cap of Liberty. The foamy rapids called Diamond Cascade are immediately below the fall. After a long curve, the river descends at a speed of 60 miles an hour to form the Silver Apron. Quieting down, it gathers into the Emerald Pool. The Merced then plunges down into the lower canyon as the Vernal Fall reaches the valley floor. To the right rises Mt. Clark, and beyond, the outlines of the Sierras.

Overhanging Rocks. That 10-foot-wide ledge of rock at the upper right-hand corner has tempted daredevils for years. The cliff below falls straight down for nearly 1,500 feet. These rocks lie on the crest of Glacier Point. At the left rises the rounded contour of Half Dome, which slopes into the Little Yosemite Valley. That tiny white line below the Overhanging Rocks is the edge of Vernal Fall. Beyond lies the snow-capped Sierras, stretching nearly 200 miles along the eastern horizon. Some of the highest mountains are 50 to 75 miles away.

Northwest from the Summit of Cloud's Rest. This view is from the summit of Cloud's Rest (9,912 feet above the sea level) looking north. The highest peaks, Mt. Lyell, Mt. Dana, and Mt. Gibbs, are on the right. At the left, below Cloud's Rest, lies Tenaya Canyon and Tenaya Lake. Behind the lake rises Tenaya Peak, and left of it, Mt. Hoffman. To the right of the lake the sharp outline of Cathedral Peak appears, and beyond lies the Tuolumne Meadows (8,500 feet).

Yosemite Falls from Glacier Point Trail. Before Yosemite Creek falls over the edge of the cliff, it rushes through a narrow cut more than 100 feet deep and about 30 feet wide. The cliff has a brilliant polish worn by the glacier that once ground its way here into the valley. The horseback party stopped on the trail has been climbing for one hour and will need two more hours to reach the top.

Half Dome from Glacier Point Trail. About two-thirds of the way up the Glacier Point Trail, Tenaya Canyon appears to the northeast, and to the right rises Half Dome. The north face is cut by a vertical fracture about 2,000 feet deep. On the back it slopes in a helmet curve into the Little Yosemite Valley. Half Dome has an altitude of 8,927 feet, that is 4,737 feet above the valley. Beyond it rises Cloud's Rest 1,000 feet higher. To the left of the canyon is Mt. Watkins at 8,200 feet high, and the crag ending the canyon is Washington Column (5,856 feet), a spur of North Dome. Mirror Lake is visible in the distance. The deep valley was carved by part of the vast Tuolumne Glacier. Deflected by Mt. Hoffman, the glacier flowed down over the summit creating these rounded domes.

From Eagle Peak, over the Valley to Glacier Point. This perspective is from the summit of Eagle Peak at 4,000 feet, the highest of the Three Brothers. The most prominent peak is Mt. Clark, nearly 11,000 feet in height. On the right is the zigzag trail leading up the cliff to Glacier Point. The Overhanging Rocks are at the very top of that triangular bluff. The valley is a mile wide at this end. The Merced River enters the valley through the canyon of the same name and drops to form Vernal and Nevada waterfalls. Nevada Fall is to the right of the Cap of Liberty, and Vernal Fall is hidden and barely visible from here.

The Wawona Road in the Valley. This view is about halfway between Inspiration Point and Bridalveil Fall. The fall is more than a mile distant, but the lacy effect of the falling waters floating in the breeze is obvious. Early in the season, the fall is 60 to 70 feet wide, but it narrows dramatically by late summer. To the left is El Capitan, and beyond, rises the rounded form of North Dome. The stagecoach (in the right corner) left Wawona on a five-hour journey to the Sentinel Hotel. Passengers relied on the skill of the four horse stage drivers on this narrow road. Accidents rarely occurred.

El Capitan Looking up the Valley to Half Dome. From the Big Oak Flat Road, El Capitan's cliffs soar upward over 3,000 feet. The Indians called it "Chief of the Valley." A little west of El Capitan, the Ribbon Fall or Virgin's Tears leaps 2,000 feet from the cliffs. Half Dome lies in the distance, near the right edge of the image.

Illilouette Fall and Canyon. About a mile down the trail from Glacier Point to Nevada Fall, this perspective looks north over the Illilouette Fall—which means "beautiful" in the Indian dialect—and down the Illilouette Canyon. Directly in front is the rounded summit of Grizzly Peak. Between Grizzly Peak and the cliff to the left lies Merced Canyon. Illilouette Canyon and the Merced unite at the foot of Grizzly Peak. From here only the upper half of Illilouette Fall is visible. The total drop, including the rapids below, makes a plunge of about 600 feet.

Mirror Lake at Sunrise. The aptly named Mirror Lake reflects the encircling mountains on its motionless surface. The lake is only 200 yards in width, but it reflects the mirrored forms of four great mountains. On the left is part of the eastern slope of North Dome, further back is the bald top of Mt. Watkins (8,200 feet), and to the right lies Cloud's Rest and the beginnings of the lower rise of Half Dome. The old Indian name for these tranquil waters was "Sleeping Water."

Going up the Zig Zags on the Steep Trail to the Top of the Nevada Fall. This party of tourists is on the Zig Zag trail to Glacier Point. Here the turns of the zig zags run up against walls of rock, but in many cases the turns occur at the very edge of a precipice, so that a horse's head often projects over a cliff of several hundred feet in making one of these sharp turns. The trail animals are so well-trained and cautious that not one serious accident has occurred. Skill in riding is not essential in these trips, for the mule left to himself will pick his way with the greatest steadiness and sagacity. Just above here, the trail forks to the left, leading to Cloud's Rest, while the Glacier Point trail turns to the right.

From Inspiration Point (east northeast) Through Yosemite Valley. The waterfall pouring over Cathedral Rocks at the south (right) looks like a slender ribbon, but it is 40 feet wide, and its waters plunge 900 feet to break into sparkles on the rocks below. That enormous bulk of a mountain beyond the Cathedral Rocks is called the Sentinel, and the height still farther away, rounded on one side and abruptly cut off on the other, is known as Half Dome. That gigantic, square shoulder of bare granite at the left (north) is El Capitan. Its summit is five-eighths of a mile above the valley. The river is coming west to meet the San Joaquin.

El Capitan with Half Dome in the Distance. The most striking object in the valley is El Capitan. It is not the highest formation, but its dominant position, majestic form, and the verticality of its face, all add up to an imposing obstacle in the narrow valley. The south and west faces of this huge granite rock join almost at right angles. The summit cannot be reached without an arduous climb. Off to the far lower right rises Half Dome (4,972 feet).

Looking Down 3,200 Feet from the Overhanging Rocks at Glacier Point to the Valley Below. On the extreme upper left is the Merced River, running south across the valley to make a great loop. A white bridge is distinctly visible against the dark water. The road to the right leads to the Happy Isles and the Merced Canyon. About 100 yards from the road, rows of white tents are among the trees. This is Camp Curry, where many tourists stayed during their visit to Yosemite.

El Capitan, 3,300 Feet High. El Capitan ("the captain") is like no other mountain cliff in the world. The cliff has two faces, the western one meeting the cliff face in the image at almost right angles. As severe and threatening as the cliff face appears, it harbors hundreds of tiny rock gardens of wild flowers almost continually in bloom, in nooks and crannies among the crevices on its face.

28

Nevada Fall and the Cap of Liberty. This view is directly opposite the Cap of Liberty on the highest point of the trail leading from Vernal Fall. Nevada Fall (right), more than a half mile away from this point, plunges in one glorious fall of 600 feet. The Indians gave it the name of "Twisting Water." The seamless rock of the Cap of Liberty bears the unmistakable marks of glacial polish on the side above the falls.

The Overhanging Rocks at Glacier Point, 3,350 Feet Above the Valley. That 10-foot-wide ledge of rock at the upper right-hand corner has tempted daredevils for years. The cliff below falls straight down for nearly 1,500 feet. These rocks lie on the crest of Glacier Point. At the left rises the rounded contour of Half Dome. That tiny white line below the Overhanging Rocks is the edge of Vernal Fall. Beyond lies the snow-capped Sierras, stretching nearly 200 miles along the eastern horizon. Some of the highest mountains are 50 to 75 miles away.

El Capitan Looking up the Valley to Half Dome. From the Big Oak Flat Road, El Capitan's cliffs soar upward over 3,000 feet. The Indians called it "Chief of the Valley." Half Dome lies in the distance, near the right edge of the image. In the left corner of the image is a clear depiction of the bulk of the talus from the face of El Capitan which dwarfs the buggy in the forefront.

Mirror Lake, Where Nature Multiplies Her Charms. This is the point where Tenaya Creek gathers into a small lake. There is no room for a large one in this hemmed-in gully. Such transparent water is not found, except in this wonderful valley. The water off the Sierra has a clearness all its own. (Mirror Lake is silting in and has lost much of its wonderful clarity. Eventually, the small lake will evolve into a meadow.)

The Stupendous El Capitan. From the edge of the Merced River rises the great granite cliff of El Capitan, the Indians' "Chief of the Valley." This massive rock wall soars upward, 3,300 feet from the valley floor. "El Cap" has intrigued climbers and artists since its discovery.

Yosemite Valley from Inspiration Point. The whole sweep of the Yosemite Valley is visible from this point on the road to Inspiration Point, about 1,500 feet above the valley. To the left is El Capitan, rising to a height of 3,300 feet from the valley. On the right is Bridalveil, falling in charming cascades to the valley. The rocks in back of the fall are called the Three Graces, but from the upper end of the valley, they are known as Cathedral Rocks. In the distance, left of Sentinel Rock, is Half Dome, and beyond that is Cloud's Rest.

Looking Down the Trail at the Beautiful Vernal Fall. From the trail up Merced Canyon appears this view of Vernal Fall. At the brink, the river is about 80 feet wide and plunges down to the rocks 350 feet below. The Indians called it the "Cataract of Diamonds." Vernal Fall is twice as high as Niagara, though obviously much narrower. All this beauty is set against the background of the rocky canyon, whose walls rise 3,000 or 4,000 feet in some places.

The Valley From Union Point. This is a western view down the valley from Union Point, about two-thirds of the way up, on the Glacier Point trail. Glacier Point is about 900 feet higher. The rock in shadows at the left is Sentinel Rock, which is over 3,000 feet above the valley. Directly down the valley are Cathedral Rocks and Spires, and the edge of El Capitan appears at the right.

Looking West from Nevada Fall Trail, Down Merced Canyon to Glacier Point. This view is from the trail leading to Nevada Fall and looking west down the Merced Canyon. The cliff rising on the right is part of the Cap of Liberty. The cliff directly in front at the end of the canyon is a part of Yosemite's south wall, which ends in Sentinel Dome. On the rocky bluff straight ahead is Glacier Point. The trail skirts along the slopes of Grizzly Peak into Yosemite Valley.

From Cloud's Rest, Southeast Over the Little Yosemite to Mt. Clark. This perspective is looking southeast from the summit of Cloud's Rest, at a height of 9,912 feet. On the left is the silvery streak of the Merced River. In front, the tallest and sharpest peak is Mt. Clark at 10,940 feet, and beyond it lie the headwaters of the San Joaquin River.

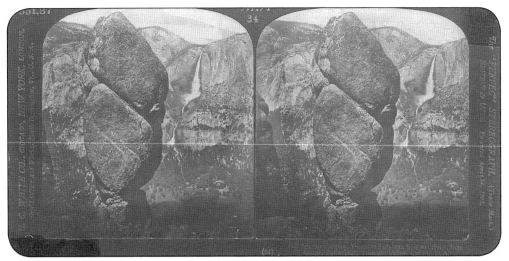

The Agassiz Column and Yosemite Falls. Named for Louis Agassiz, North America's glacial expert at the time and paradoxically a staunch anti-evolutionist, the column is 85 feet in height and stands on a narrow base. The hotel below in the lower right-hand corner is the Sentinel. Yosemite Falls thunder in the distance.

The Fallen Monarch at Mariposa Grove with the 15th U.S. Cavalry. The bulk of this huge tree is aptly demonstrated by comfortably accommodating the men and mounts of the 15th U.S. Cavalry, Troop I. By the mid-1890s, U.S. Cavalry troops were established in the national parks to police restricted areas and maintain order.

Grizzly Giant. In Mariposa Grove, the largest grove of giant Sequoia trees outside of Sequoia National Park, is the Grizzly Giant with a base diameter of 34 feet and a height of 209 feet. A great many people have posed in front of this tree, from presidents to venerable naturalists.

Fallen Monarch. This is one of the atypical views of the Fallen Monarch, surrounded by lesser trees in the Mariposa Grove. It is most frequently photographed in ways that enhance the height and circumference, implying that it stands in isolated grandeur rather than in forested surroundings. This image illustrates why the giant trees went undiscovered for as long as they did.

1214. Glacier Point from Nevada Falls Trail, Yosemite Valley, California

North Dome, 3,568 Feet High. Although the following two views look like photographic images when viewed through a stereoscope, they are not. They are hand-tinted prints derived from photographic images and "enhanced" by an artist and the printing process. This is an early attempt to produce a view of Yosemite in color.

1208. North Dome (3,568 feet high), Yosemite, Cal.

Glacier Point From Nevada Fall Trail, Yosemite Valley. Compare this with the first image on page 33, from a similar vantage point on the Nevada Fall Trail.

Two

SCENIC VIEWS

The massive peaks, cliffs, and domes of Yosemite are a large part of what makes the park a world-class attraction. In the early years of the park, there was great controversy over how Yosemite was created, but with scientific analysis and observation, geologists have discovered that it was formed over millions of years by plate tectonics, glaciation, and exfoliation. At one time, the area was covered by a shallow sea that became a valley of rolling hills. Movement in the earth's crust (plate tectonics) lifted and tilted huge sections of land that created mountain ranges, while the Merced River cut a canyon through the area. During the various Ice Ages, glaciers further sculpted the terrain, cutting through all but the hardiest granite. The glaciers also covered most of the domes we know of today but didn't shape them into the rounded forms we see. That was created by a process called "exfoliation," where sheets of rock fall away due to pressure and outward expansion of the rock. The rounded shape occurs because exfoliation tends to break off sharp corners.

Four Famous Views in Yosemite Valley. [FCL]

El Capitan—the Whole View.
Originally called To-to'-kon oolah by
the Ahwahneeches after a chief named
To-to'-kon (meaning "sandhill crane"),
Dr. Bunnell of the Mariposa Battalion
renamed the cliff El Capitan, because he
misinterpreted To-to'-kon as "rock chief."
It stands 3,464 feet above the floor of
Yosemite Valley, 2.5 times the height of the
Rock of Gibraltar and 7,564 feet above sea
level. [GG65]

A Closer Look. Over the years, El
Capitan has provided a challenge for
many a rock climber. [GG39]

EL CAPITAN, YOSEMITE NATIONAL PARK

El Cap—Framed in White. As one of the park's most famous sights, El Capitan has been extensively photographed from all angles and in all seasons. [GG64]

306　HALF DOME FROM THE FLOOR OF THE VALLEY　84346

Half Dome. Half Dome, or South Dome, as it used to be called, was given the name Tis-sa-ack (Goddess of the Valley) by the Miwoks. It is, of course, best known for its sheer, flat façade on one side, hence its present name. Long a source of wonder and awe, Half Dome was never one full dome like North Dome. At some point, the granite from its north side broke off in vertical sheets due to movement of a glacier through Tenaya Canyon. [FCL]

Pillsbury's Half Dome. This sepia-tone photograph of Half Dome was taken by Arthur Pillsbury, c. 1925. [GG42]

11511 HALF DOME AND HIGH SIERRAS, YOSEMITE VALLEY, CALIF.

Scaling Half Dome. In 1875, blacksmith George C. Anderson was the first man to attempt climbing Half Dome. Anderson made iron eyebolts that he fastened to wooden pegs driven into holes he drilled in order to create footholds on the back side of the cliff. For several years, there was a rope ladder that both men and women used, although it eventually rotted away. Today, scaling Half Dome is achieved by using an anchored "staircase" made of metal cables. [GG67]

YOSEMITE NATIONAL PARK

326 WASHINGTON COLUMN AND HALF DOME FROM MERCED RIVER

Wish you were Here. This postcard was mailed from Camp Curry in the park in 1941. [GG9]

41

346 HALF DOME AND CLOUD'S REST, AS SEEN FROM GLACIER POINT

Another View of Half Dome with Cloud's Rest. The back of this postcard reads: "This huge dome dominates the eastern end of the valley and has an elevation of 8,852 feet above sea level, rising 4,941 feet above the floor of the valley. The face of it is cut sheer and noticeably concave for approximately 2,000 feet. Cloud's Rest, in the distance, is 9,924 feet high" (from sea level, 5594 feet from the valley floor). [FCL]

The Sierra Nevadas from Eagle Peak showing Clowds Rest, Half Dome and Glacier Point. Yosemite Valley. Califor

Glacier Point. Glacier Point is a popular scenic lookout where the famous overhanging rock resides. [GG23]

Cathedral Rocks (Three Graces). The Cathedral Rocks sit next to the Cathedral Spires and opposite El Capitan in Yosemite Valley. They rise to 2,591 feet and were once called the Three Graces, because as seen from the west, they have a very different appearance. [GG35]

An Early Hand-Tinted Card. The message on the back of this postcard reads: "Mirrored in a beautiful lake, surrounded by a variety of tall pines, oaks, and heavy woods, the Cathedral Rocks stand out boldly from the surrounding country. It is one, if not the greatest sights, of all the wonderful spots of the Yosemite Valley." [FCL]

Cathedral Spires, 2200 feet, Yosemite, Cal.

Cathedral Spires. So named because of its resemblance to a Gothic cathedral, each of the peaks towers above the valley floor at an impressive height. The right spire is 2,678 feet tall, and the left is 2,579 feet tall. It even inspired a poem:

The Spires
No foot has pressed those stairways dizzy,
No hand has touched those silent bells;
No mortal sacristan there busy,
Silence alone the story tells,
Those aisles untrod, save by the spirits,
Whose mortal forms rest 'neath the sod;
They only have the power to hear its
Chimes of God.

—C.W. Kyle

(*Foley's Yosemite Souvenir and Guide*, Yosemite, California: Foley's Studio, [7th ed, 1905], p. 39) [GG32]

Three Brothers. The three overlapping peaks known as Three Brothers were originally called Kom-po-pai-zes or Pompomposus, loosely translated by Dr. Bunnell as "mountains playing leapfrog." It was allegedly named Three Brothers because three of Chief Tenaya's sons were captured near the peaks by the Mariposa Battalion. [GG70]

Cap of Liberty. Although not as well known as other peaks, the Cap of Liberty has had a colorful history, at least in its naming. It has been called Mt. Frances, Gwin's Peak, Bellow's Butte, and Mt. Broderick. As legend has it, in 1865, Leland Stanford, railroad baron and then governor of California, renamed the peak because he disliked its former names and thought the peak resembled the cap of liberty on a half-dollar coin. [FCL]

An Artistic, Photographic Postcard from Camp Curry Studio. [FCL]

Mirror Lake. Mirror Lake is a small but often photographed lake in the mouth of Tenaya Canyon, so named because of the glass-like reflections it provides of Mount Watkins, the Royal Arches, Washington Column, and Three Brothers. Because of its often still, unbroken surface, its Miwok name was purportedly Ke-ko-too-yem or "sleeping waters." [GG72]

307   Royal Arches, Washington Column and Half Dome   84347

One Large Edifice. The back of this postcard reads: "The Royal Arches at the east end of the valley are in a steep vertical wall whose summit is the North Dome, Washington Column being the angle of this wall." [FCL]

1432 — North Dome, Washington Column and Royal Arches, Yosemite Valley, California.

Royal Arches, Washington Column, and the Domes. Distinguished by its sculpted, semi-circular indentations, the Royal Arches are often shown with Washington Column (1,952 feet tall) and North Dome (3,571 feet). The Arches stand opposite the famed Glacier Point, while Washington Column sits in the middle at the juncture between Tenaya Canyon and Yosemite Valley. North Dome graces the north side of Tenaya Canyon. The length rather than the height of the Royal Arches is what makes it impressive, measured at a quarter of a mile or 1,800 feet long. [GG68]

49

A Serene Winter Scene. This postcard dates from c. 1911, affording its recipients what would have been, at that time, a rare glimpse of Yosemite in the winter. [FCL]

The Fissures. The popular vantage point known as the Fissures or Profile Cliff is east of Taft Point. This gorge was formed by seeping water weakening cracks within the rock and causing chunks to break off. Depending on the time of day and lighting, different silhouettes can be seen on the rock. [GG13]

Old Inspiration Point. Old Inspiration Point is 2,500 feet from the floor of Yosemite Valley and is said to be the vantage point from which the Mariposa Battalion first saw the valley. [GG80]

A Bas-Relief Postcard. A view from Inspiration Point, this postcard has an unusual three-dimensional effect due to its raised (bas-relief) surface. [GG24]

305   HAPPY ISLES, YOSEMITE VALLEY   3A-H159

Happy Isles. The message on the back of the postcard reads: "At this point just below the Vernal Fall, the turbulent waters of the Merced, hemmed in a rock-walled canyon, dash madly about these little isles."

Called Island Rapids by James Hutchings, one of the pioneer residents of Yosemite, it was renamed Happy Isles by W.E. Deninson, guardian of Yosemite Valley, because "no one can visit them without for the while forgetting the grinding strife of his world and being happy." [FCL]

Wawona Tunnel. Wawona means "big tree," an appropriate name for the road that leads to the Mariposa Grove of Big Trees. For many visitors, this vista is their first view of Yosemite Valley. [FCL]

Tioga Pass. Tioga Pass, at a maximum elevation of 9,945 feet, is the apex of Tioga Road, the highest road in California and one of its most diverse in alpine scenery. It has the distinction of passing by peaks and domes, lakes, forests, meadows, and flowering rock gardens on the west side, but once past the Tioga Pass, the landscape becomes more arid, with steep cliffs and ravines. Once called the Great Sierra Wagon Road, completed in 1883 by Chinese laborers working for the Great Sierra Consolidated Silver Mining Company, the road had become abandoned by 1915 but was reopened by the federal government as a public throughway in 1919. [GG6]

Three

GETTING THERE AND STAYING A WHILE

Before the Yosemite Valley Railroad was completed, the tourist who wished to see the grandeur of Yosemite was forced to endure an expensive and grueling two-day trip by stage and horseback. Once the Yosemite-bound visitor left San Francisco, he or she was subjected to hours on horse or mule, days and nights in a bone-rattling, backbreaking stagecoach over some of the worst roads and terrains imaginable. The railroad was a huge improvement for the poor tourist who had formerly been subject to a punishing trip before the glories of Yosemite made all the ills of travel worthwhile.

The "Short line to Paradise" was completed in 1907 at an estimated cost of just over $4 million. Passengers boarded the train at Merced and detrained after a comfortable four-hour journey with all the amenities at El Portal. The park's early management forbade automobiles, so visitors completed the 12 miles into Yosemite Valley by horse-drawn vehicle. Several small villages and hamlets were on the train route. Snelling, Merced Falls, Exchequer, Bagby, Briceburg, and Incline were often stops along the way until the tourist reached El Portal, the end of the Yosemite Valley Railroad line.

The Yosemite Valley Railroad's safety record was not spotless. There were a couple of accidents, crew members were killed, and tourists were injured, but overall, the railroad was instantly popular and a much safer and more comfortable ride than earlier modes of transportation.

Yosemite Valley Railroad Depot, Merced, California. The Yosemite Valley Railroad was headquartered in Merced. Both Santa Fe and Southern Pacific railroad lines came into Merced from Los Angeles and San Francisco, making the quiet valley town the obvious jumping-off place for the Yosemite adventure. The station was gutted by fire in 1929, and its duplicate was rebuilt on the same site. [FCL]

Train Above Merced Falls, West of Yosemite. Merced Falls was a station located in the rolling hills just about 24 miles out of Merced. A post office was established there in 1856 and was closed in 1957. A large lumber mill operation was built and flourished in the 1920s. This is the point on the route where the train enters into Merced Canyon. This card was mailed in 1911. [FCL]

Bridge Below Bagby, in the Merced River Canyon, En Route to Yosemite. Bagby was a settlement in Mariposa County about 48 miles out of Merced. Bagby was named for an early resident who ran the local hotel and saloon; the site is now covered by the waters of Lake McClure. [FCL]

Merced Canyon on Yosemite Valley Railroad Line. This card was mailed in August of 1917, but the image dates from about ten years earlier. The engine matches the profile of Engine #23, which was built in 1907 and cost just under $15,000. The Yosemite Valley Railroad followed the scenic Merced River for the large majority of the 78-mile route. [FCL]

Box Canyon En Route to Yosemite.
Here the Merced River finds its way
through a narrow channel worn through
the solid rock one hundred feet below.
Postcard views were often sent to
Germany to be hand-tinted and printed
less expensively as were the Yosemite
Valley Railroad cards in this series. [FCL]

Merced Canyon, the Approach to Yosemite Valley. The Yosemite Valley Railroad
provided, for $18.50, a 78-mile-long steel highway, complete with observation cars,
dining cars, and Pullmans, through some of California's most scenic country—the
$18.50 included the stagecoach ride from El Portal to the valley floor. [FCL]

The Portal, thro' Arch of Oaks, in the Merced River Canyon, en route to Yosemite, Cal.

Portal of Oaks. Just one of the very attractive scenes that entertained tourists as the train cut its way through the terrain of Merced Canyon, Yosemite had now become accessible to more than just the hardiest and most determined tourist. This was the beginning of Yosemite's reign as one of the crown jewels of the United States' National Parks. The valley's infinite attraction is both a saving grace and a danger. Park management balances a fine line between access and overuse each season to the delight and dismay of tourists. [GG34]

El Portal, the End of the Line. This rustic station was the end of the line for the Yosemite Valley Railroad. Passengers detrained at El Portal, the easternmost point on the Yosemite Valley Railroad, and began the hour-and-a-half stage trip into Yosemite Valley. Later, touring cars carried visitors over the remaining 12 miles into the valley. [FCL]

El Portal Station. This second view of the railroad terminus at El Portal Station is from the large covered waiting area looking toward the actual station. The backs of benches are visible at the lower right corner. Tourists waited here in the station for stages and cars to the valley floor. The station was in continual use during the summer season. The large covered area served to load and disembark visitors in inclement weather and provided shelter when the station was filled to capacity. [FCL]

The Del Portal Hotel, El Portal, California. The four-story Del Portal Hotel was built in 1907 by the Yosemite Terminal Company for about $50,000. It contained a restaurant and dining room which could serve over a hundred persons at one sitting. Thirty of its one hundred fifty rooms had private baths. It was situated on the bluff, 2,000 feet above the Merced River. The Del Portal burned on October 27, 1917, and the building was declared a total loss. [FCL]

Wawona Hotel, on the Road of a Thousand Wonders. Established in 1856 on the site of Galen Clark's first station, the Wawona Hotel went through many incarnations until it was purchased by the Washburn family. Mrs. Washburn named the hotel Wawona in 1884. The meaning of the name has had various interpretations, but "big tree" seems to be the most likely. [FCL]

Are We There Yet? Situated between stage stops en route to Yosemite, the Wawona Hotel offered weary tourists a welcome respite from the rattle and shake of stage travel. The idyllic setting depicted on this card illustrates how inviting the Wawona must have appeared to the early tourist. It still offers visitors its own brand of tranquility and charm. [FCL]

Sentinel Hotel, Yosemite Valley. In 1863, James M. Hutchings bought and began renovations on the Upper Hotel. It became the Sentinel Hotel and was operated by the Hutchings family until 1874, when the park purchased the privately-owned land. [FCL]

The Sentinel Hotel in Winter. The Sentinel in snow captures the grace and special charm of Yosemite in winter. The hush of snow adds serenity and stillness to enhance the majesty of the hotel's surroundings. This image was taken by Arthur Pillsbury, resident Yosemite photographer. By 1925, when this card was mailed, plans were made to replace the Sentinel with a more modern hotel. [GG2]

The Ahwahnee Hotel Amid Yosemite's Grandeur. Opened to the public on July 14, 1927, the world-class Ahwahnee Hotel was the first year-round hotel in Yosemite. It was built on the original site of Kenney's stable and stagecoach operation. Architect G.S. Underwood's hotel appears to be a child of the cliffs themselves. [FCL]

The Ahwahnee Hotel with Some of Yosemite's Residents. The Ahwahnee has played host to hundreds of thousands of park visitors during its long tenure as the Park's *grande doyenne*. Its name is derived from the name of the earliest tribe that settled in the Yosemite Valley, the Ahwaneechees. Some say the hotel name translates to "deep grassy meadow." [FCL]

THE AHWAHNEE HOTEL · YOSEMITE

The Fabulous Ahwahnee. The Ahwahnee Hotel, with its first cornerstone laid in August of 1926, is famous worldwide for its hospitality and breathtaking vistas. Most of the building materials—sugar pine and flagstone—were milled and mined locally. This excludes the 680 tons of structural steel used in framing the structure. [GG75]

The Yosemite Lodge. The new Yosemite Lodge complex, composed largely of four redwood buildings with expansive use of glass, was built from 1954 to 1955, and opened for the tourist season in June of 1956. The former Yosemite Lodge was used as army quarters and barracks before renovation. [GG74]

Camp Curry. Foster Curry designed this rustic gate for his parents, David and Jennie Curry, at their campground. Camp Curry began as a fledgling enterprise in 1899 and grew into a huge industry. The Curry family hosted Yosemite guests for decades. Both the family and the camp were considered park fixtures. [GG76]

A Room with a View in the Great Outdoors. Comfortable lodging in Yosemite could be had at the "tent hotel" known as Camp Curry for $12 a week. This was more reasonable for those unaccustomed to the higher rates of Yosemite's hotels. The business flourished. [FCL]

The Scenic Route—Travel by Stagecoach. This card depicts the arrival of tourists to Yosemite Valley by stagecoach. This group probably arrived at El Portal Station on the Yosemite Valley Railroad and made the last leg of the journey in the comfort of an open stagecoach, which traveled about 8 miles per hour. For a long while, automobiles were forbidden entry into the park, whether this was an effort to maintain the park's pristine quality or a bias is unknown. Cars were finally allowed into the park in late August of 1913. [FCL]

Starting for Glacier Point, Yosemite Valley. This tourist party is mounted on mules and horses for the climb up to Glacier Point. The saddle stock was carefully selected for levelheadedness and surefootedness. Very few accidents occurred, despite the fact that tourists came to the park with hugely varied levels of equestrian skills. Mules were often the favored choice of tourists, because they were thought to be more reliable on the trail. In reality, mules are better at self preservation. [GG60]

Camp Yosemite. Camp Yosemite or Camp Lost Arrow as it was later named, was begun in 1901 by the Washburn family, who also owned and managed the Wawona Hotel. The camp was permanently closed when the first Yosemite Lodge opened in 1915. [FCL]

Camp Ahwahnee. Camp Ahwahnee, another tent campground for tourists, was begun in direct competition with Camp Curry in 1908. It was operated by the Sell family. This card was mailed on July 25, 1912. [GG48]

CAMP CURRY'S FIRE FALL.

Camp Curry's Firefall. Each night during the summer season, a huge bonfire was built on Glacier Point, 3,200 feet directly above Camp Curry. At the conclusion of the nightly campfire entertainment, generally between 9 and 9:30 p.m., the glittering coals were pushed over the point, and the man-made cataract of fire, sparks, and embers made a sheer drop over 2,000 feet to fall harmlessly below for the enjoyment of the guests looking up in the campground. [FCL and GG77]

A Special Luminous Postcard. Due to a revision of park policy, the last firefall fell from Glacier Point on January 25, 1968. While not in keeping with the park's natural attractions, the firefall was a tourist favorite and is remembered with awe and nostalgia by those fortunate enough to have seen it. The first was probably begun by James Hutchings as a tourist attraction, although some sources have credited James McCauley with the first firefall in the 1860s. The tradition died out and was later resurrected by David Curry. It succeeded in impressing tourists intermittently for years. This card is so treated that when exposed to bright light, it will glow in the dark. [FCL and GG78]

Four

FABULOUS FALLS

The park is justifiably famous for its spectacular waterfalls, which have long been a source of wonder and awe for tourists since the park's inception and before for the Native Americans who inhabited the area. The falls have been photographed, painted, and paid homage to in countless ways. Ranging in height from 325 to 2,425 feet, the falls are most spectacular in the spring, after the snowmelt in the mountains. But by late summer, especially in dry years, the flow can be no more than a trickle.

Five Famous Waterfalls. Would Yosemite be as renowned without its wonderful waterfalls? [GG61]

Yosemite Falls. At a total height of 2,425 feet, Yosemite Falls is one of the world's highest and the park's most famous waterfall. It is actually comprised of three cascades. The upper fall plunges down 1,430 feet in an unbroken plummet (equivalent to nine Niagara Falls end to end), while the lower two falls drop another 675 feet and 320 feet, respectively. The original Miwok Indian name for the fall was Choo-look or Scholook, meaning simply "the fall." [FCL]

"Fall" or "Falls"? Yosemite Falls is sometimes referred to as Yosemite Fall (as this postcard does) even though there are actually three falls that comprise Yosemite Falls. [GG56]

The Grandeur of Yosemite Falls by A. Pillsbury. [GG43]

YOSEMITE FALLS, Mariposa County, Calif., comprising three falls. The first is 1,500 feet high, the second 626 feet in a series of cascades, and the third 400 feet high.

From a Stereograph. This postcard was a promotional item from the Prudential Insurance Company, using an image from a 1902 Underwood and Underwood stereograph. [GG55]

YOSEMITE FALLS, YOSEMITE NATIONAL PARK, CALIFORNIA
REACHED VIA UNION PACIFIC RAILROAD

Union Pacific Railroad. The message on the back of this postcard reads: "The Union Pacific runs fast de luxe [sic] trains daily to California via the scenic and historic Overland Route." (Permission to use courtesy of the Union Pacific Railroad.) [FCL]

73

Vernal Falls, Yosemite National Park

Discreet Advertising, Brought to You by... The back of the postcard reads: "Written from a Telephone Center provided by the Pacific Telephone and Telegraph Company." [GG57]

An Incessant Baptism. The message on the back of this postcard reads: "The river is nearly 90 feet wide here and drops straight down 350 feet. The spray is driven outward like smoke, and everything of plant and grass, moss and fern is kept green by the incessant baptism." [GG31]

Vernal Fall. Dr. Bunnell anointed Vernal Fall with its name because, in his own words, "cool, moist air and newly-springing Kentucky bluegrass, at the Vernal, with the sun shining through the spray, as in an April shower, suggested the sensation of spring." There is some debate over what its original name was, but Yan-o-pah, "little cloud" or "mist," is most commonly accepted. [GG58]

Nevada Fall. Originally called Yo-wi-ye by the Miwok tribe, Nevada ("snow-covered") Fall was named by Dr. Lafayette Bunnell, a physician with the Mariposa Battalion in 1851. It sits above Vernal Fall along the Merced River, and is said to have reminded Bunnell of an avalanche of snow. [GG1]

The Auto-Chrom Method. This is a Goeggel and Weidner postcard printed in Germany (c. 1905) using the Auto-Chrom method, whereby a halftone screen with black ink details are laid over lithographed colors. [GG21]

YOSEMITE NATIONAL PARK

315   BRIDAL VEIL FALL, YOSEMITE VALLEY   3A-H161

Bridalveil Fall. The romantically named Bridalveil Fall drops in a sheer cascade of water for 600 feet. The prevalent wind frequently catches the great plume of water and drifts it across the face of the cliff, much like a veil. This is one of the most popular spots in the park for both planned and impromptu marriage proposals. One of the few falls not named by Dr. Bunnell, it was named in 1856 by Warren Baer, then editor of the *Mariposa Democrat.* [FCL]

Five

BIG TREES

Giant sequoia (*Sequoia gigantean)* are often confused with its cousins, the giant redwoods (*Sequoia sempervirens*). What adds to the confusion is the fact that giant sequoia are sometimes called Sierra redwoods. Both types grow in California, but the true redwoods are found along the coast while the sequoia exist only in discrete, isolated groves on the western slope of the Sierra Nevada, at elevations between 5,000 and 8,000 feet. Redwoods are taller, but sequoia are thicker. As a species, sequoia are the world's largest living things whose ancestry can be traced back 200 million years. Official discovery and widespread public awareness of the giant sequoia occurred in 1852, when a canal company hunter, Augustus T. Dowd, came upon them in the Calaveras Grove, northwest of the Yosemite area. James Hutchings described the discovery in several publications. In one he wrote: "But a short time was allowed to elapse after the discovery of this remarkable grove before the trumpet-tongued press proclaimed the wonder to all sections of the state, and to all parts of the world, and the lovers of the marvelous began first to doubt, then to believe, and afterwards to flock to see with their own eyes the objects of which they had heard so much." The trees were such a curiosity that a 20-foot cross-section was sent to the 1876 Centennial Exhibition in Philadelphia but was considered by many to be a hoax.

There are three sequoia groves within the park's boundaries—Mariposa, Tuolumne, and Merced Groves. Mariposa Grove, with about five hundred mature sequoias, near the southern entrance to the park, is the largest, most accessible, and therefore most frequently visited grove. On the western edge of the park, Tuolumne Grove is much smaller, with 25 sequoias. Merced Grove, near Tuolumne Grove, is the smallest of the groves and the last to be discovered in 1870 during a wagon road survey. It is also the most inaccessible, seen only by hikers.

The Grizzly Giant. [FCL]

The Grizzly Giant and the Cavalry. Located near the southwestern entrance to the park, the Mariposa Big Tree Grove, famous for its massive Sequoias (the largest, oldest trees in the world), was first discovered by a hunter, Mr. Ogg, in 1855. The largest tree in the Lower Grove is the Grizzly Giant, with a circumference of 92 feet, 7 inches and a diameter of 31 feet at its base, a fact emphasized by this troop of cavalrymen surrounding the tree.

The Grizzly Giant encompasses more than 30,000 cubic feet and stands at 209 feet. It is also one of the oldest trees in the park, estimated to be between 2,700 to more than 3,800 years old. At one time, the tree stood much taller, but lightning has hit the Grizzly Giant many times over its long history and decreased its stature but not its vigor. It leans at a 17-degree angle and used to be secured by cables for fear that it would topple over. Now, however, it is left in its natural state, to stand and eventually fall. [GG16]

Yosemite's First Guardian. In 1864, the U.S. Congress declared the Mariposa Grove of Big Trees and Yosemite Valley as scenic preserves to be managed by the state of California. The preserve was called the Yosemite Grant, and Galen Clark became its first guardian, a position he held off and on for 30 years. Clark built a log cabin in the Mariposa Grove. The site of the original cabin is now where the Grove Museum stands. [GG11]

Clark's Ranch. Galen Clark built his log cabin not just for himself but for visitors to Yosemite as well. First called Clark's Station, he later enlarged his cabin and renamed it Clark's Ranch. One guest described him as "one of those men one frequently meets in California—the modern anchorite—a hater of civilization and a lover of the forest—handsome, thoughtful, interesting, and slovenly." Others simply remember him as kind, hospitable, honest, witty, and wise. [GG14]

Fallen Monarch. One of the most famous and frequently photographed of the fallen sequoias is the Fallen Monarch. The date of its fall is unknown, but some of the earliest Yosemite postcards show the Fallen Monarch with various people and equipment to emphasize its immensity. [FCL]

Would Ya Look at That! In the early twentieth century, this image would have evoked much wonder and amazement. In a less jaded world, seeing men on horses standing on a tree trunk would have had great entertainment value. [FCL]

Your Roots are Showing. [GG40]

An Early Postcard, c. 1906. It's interesting to note that the handwritten message is on the front of this postcard, an example of early postcards whose backs were reserved for the recipients' and senders' addresses. The small amount of white space on the front of the postcard was the only space for a personal message. [GG49]

Just Passing Through. The Wawona Tunnel Tree was one of the park's most popular attractions. It stood at 231 feet with a circumference of 86.4 feet at its base and a diameter of 27.5 feet. Its most celebrated feature was the tunnel cut right through it. In 1881, an old burn scar in the tree was enlarged by the Scribner brothers for the Yosemite Stage and Turnpike Company. They were paid $75. The tunnel itself was 8 feet wide, 9 feet high, and 26 feet long, first traversed by wagons and later by cars. [FCL]

A Cut Above the Rest. The cut through the Wawona Tunnel Tree never affected its vitality or continued growth. It thrived for many years until it fell in 1969 during a record snowstorm. [FCL]

Meandering Through the Trees. Of course, park management no longer allows cars (or buggies) to drive amidst the sequoia, but this road used to be a very popular scenic route, traversed by many Yosemite sojourners. [GG44]

The Age of a Monarch, Mariposa Grove of Big Trees

Tree Rings. As trees mature, they increase in both height and girth. Tree-ring dating is the method by which a tree's age is determined. The more concentric rings there are in the trunk of a tree, the older it is. The rings on the stump of this fallen sequoia are shown with parallels to significant historical events. The date of the earliest ring is A.D. 919, and the latest is 1916, when the tree fell. [GG82]

Tuolumne Grove. Tuolumne Grove was one of the first stands of giant sequoia to be discovered by non-Indians. In 1833, Joseph R. Walker and his party of 60 hunters and trappers traveled across the Sierra Nevada from east to west, eventually coming upon the Tuolumne Grove and possibly the Merced Grove, on what is now the western boundary of the park. In 1835, the Walker Expedition's clerk, Zenas Leonard, wrote about the trip for his local Clearfield County, Pennsylvania, newspaper. He wrote of the trees: "In the last two days traveling, we have found some trees of the Redwood species, incredibly large—some of which would measure from 16 to 18 fathom round the trunk at the height of a man's head from the ground." [GG79]

YOSEMITE NATIONAL PARK

363   THE MASSACHUSETTS TREE   283-29

Massachusetts Tree. The back of this postcard reads: "The Massachusetts Tree is the latest sequioah [sic] to have fallen. It was standing erect and green in 1926, and was blown to earth in a windstorm in the spring of 1927." It appears that the tree is being prepared for milling, a practice no longer condoned by the National Park Service. However, in the years of extensive logging, it was common knowledge among loggers that a single sequoia tree could supply the same amount of lumber as an entire acre of Pacific Northwest forest. Although weak and brittle, sequoia wood was often used for fence posts, shingles, and grapevine stakes, because it resists decay. [GG10]

Six

ROCKS (OR POSTCARDS FROM THE LEDGE)

The Overhanging Rocks at Glacier Point have tempted daredevils and enticed tourists for decades. The ledge of rock, only 6 to 8 feet wide, juts out free from the cliff, over the valley 3,250 feet below. Whether the view inspires awe or nausea rests with the beholder. Judging from the number and variety of postcards featuring the rocks, with everything from Winky the burro, to cars, acrobats, and bickering couples, they are apparently irresistible.

The largest thing posed on the rocks was probably an automobile. Mr. Pillsbury was by no means the first to drive a vehicle onto the rocks. Oliver Lippincott drove his Locomobile to Glacier Point and onto the Overhanging Rocks in the summer of 1900.

Yosemite's Points of Interest. This card from Pillsbury's Pictures in Yosemite Valley names the points of interest as seen from Glacier Point. This is a very useful card. The geological features tend to overwhelm the average tourist, and names fade away when facing this fabulous vista. [FCL]

"Winky" at Glacier Point. It is interesting to consider how his handlers got Winky out there, but an even bigger concern is how did they get Winky turned around and back? [FCL]

Overhanging Rock at Glacier Point, 3200 feet from the floor of the Valley, Yosemite, Cal.

Overhanging Rock at Glacier Point, 3200 Feet from the Floor of the Valley. Even a handstand can't improve this view. [FCL]

Pillsbury's Studebaker Six at Glacier Point. The new Studebaker Six automobile, weighing 2,700 pounds, was owned by Arthur Pillsbury (who is seated on the hood), a Yosemite photographer who staged the shot. His party was photographed in September of 1916. [FCL]

Overhanging Rock at Glacier Point, Above the Merced. Is he holding her or pushing her? [FCL]

Weather is miserable here. Hope you are well. Folks all fine. Mae.

Anything for a Shot? This early card was mailed on August 11, 1908. Was it too hot or too wet? One hopes the intrepid photographer got his shot. [FCL]

The Valley Below the Overhanging Rock, Glacier Point. This spectacular view clearly reveals just how far the rocks "overhang," and just how far the drop would be. [FCL]

A Penny for your Thoughts. These two cards required a penny for postage to send the visual pun of Glacier "Point" home to unsuspecting friends and family. [FCL]

Glacier Point Yosemite Valley, Cal.

Get the Point? If you missed the pun in the first card, it is repeated here in case you missed "the point." [FCL]

High Kicks over the Valley. Kitty Tatch, who worked at the Sentinel Hotel, was photographed in several poses, once doing high kicks in the voluminous clothing of the 1900s. She was known for her aplomb both off and on the rocks. The card featuring the high kicker in the flat-brimmed hat is probably Kitty. [FCL]

Who Says Women are the Weaker Sex? Kitty often autographed postcards for tourists, but this card unfortunately does not have her signature or her companion's. George Fiske, a longtime Yosemite photographer, captured a similar image in a stereoview around the turn of the century. His model looked suspiciously like Kitty. [FCL]

The Thrill of Danger. Neither sleet, nor snow, rain, or summer heat could dim the charm of hanging over certain death at the slip of a boot. [FCL]

The Rock in Winter. Even during the height of winter's chill, the view from the "rock" was thrilling. The slippery ice and snow must have added a certain fillip to the danger. [FCL]

Glacier Point (overhanging Rock) and Half Dome,
Yosemite Valley, California, showing
Vernal and Nevada Falls.

Glacier Point and Half Dome Showing Vernal and Nevada Falls. This card clearly illustrates that the view was worth the climb to Glacier Point. The adrenaline rush from this perch must have made it memorable too. [FCL]

A Perilous Perch. At least this doughty mountaineer is sitting a little bit further back on this perilous perch. [FCL]

Two's Company. Tourists often found solace in dragging another person with them out onto the Rocks. [FCL]

Warning: Proceed at Your Own Risk. The sign posted expresses an early park management opinion. Now, daredevils and adventurous tourists are expressly forbidden access to the Overhanging Rocks. [FCL]

The Arch Rock. Yosemite is filled with oddities to delight the tourist, and this is one of them. Arch Rock is still a favorite passage on the way to the valley from the Mariposa County, El Portal entrance. It is a tight squeeze for all but economy model vehicles. The roadway was built by the Yosemite Valley Railroad, who did not receive any compensation for the work from either the State of California or the Parks Department. [GG71]

Tunnel Rock en Route to Yosemite Valley. The stage was the typical mode of transportation tourists used once they reached the end of the line at El Portal Station and detrained. The open-stage ride down the remaining 12 miles into the valley included a series of exhilarating vistas succeeded by awesome perspectives. [GG41]

Seven

SOUVENIR PACKETS

Souvenir packets of photographic postcards were a natural outgrowth of the popularity of both Yosemite and the photograph. By the early 1860s, photography and Yosemite were inevitably linked. The photograph was in part responsible for establishing Yosemite's credentials as one of nature's finest works. The photograph drew Congressional attention to the park in the 1860s. Carleton E. Watkins' images played an important part in encouraging Congress to set the land aside as a place of beauty "for the benefit of mankind."

In 1861, C.E. Watkins visited the Yosemite Valley. He produced the first 18 x 22-sized prints of the valley. Twelve or more mules were required to pack in Watkins's gear, and five pack animals were devoted to photographic equipment. Watkins liked to spend summers photographing California scenes, but he also photographed parts of Oregon, Nevada, and British Columbia. Watkins eventually lost his sight. He was led from the dangers of the 1906 San Francisco earthquake by his son. His collection of prints and negatives was unfortunately lost in the fire.

This souvenir folder of black and white photos of Yosemite dates from the late 1920s to the early '30s, and was manufactured and printed by Wayne Paper Box and Printing Corporation in Fort Wayne, Indiana. It opens appropriately with the world-famous view of the park from the Wawona Tunnel. This breathtaking vista is often the first view tourists have of Yosemite Valley. The Wawona Tunnel opened to the public on June 10, 1933. The 28-foot-wide, 4,230-foot-long shaft was completed in just under seven hundred days. The shaft was drilled through solid granite. [FCL and GG83]

PACK TRAIN IN HIGH SIERRAS. CALIF.   K-118

Pack Train in High Sierras. It is hard to imagine freighting in all supplies, furniture, and food to supply the early tourist with even modest amenities.

VERDANT MEADOW LOOKING TOWARD MT. SHINN, CALIF.   K-112

Verdant Meadow Looking Toward Mt. Shinn, California. This idyllic spot, and others like it, are found frequently throughout the Sierras. Mt. Shinn was named for Charles Shinn, a charter member of the Sierra Club, in 1925.

FISH CAMP, MADERA COUNTY, CALIF.   K-150

Fish Camp, Madera County, California. Fish Camp is a small hamlet located on the highway into Yosemite. It was the site of a seasonal camp for local Indians who fished and harvested acorns from the Black Oaks in the area. In 1878, Henry Washburn began his new road into Wawona. Fish Camp was a welcome stop then and now.

BRIDGE ON MERCED RIVER, YOSEMITE NATIONAL PARK, CALIF.   K-139

Bridge on Merced River, Yosemite. The placid charm of the Merced River on this card is misleading. It is actually a dangerous torrent during snowmelt, and has claimed many lives. Mirror Lake and Merced River offer many beautiful settings among the groves of trees, brilliant shrubs, and multi-colored wildflowers.

99

EL CAPITAN, YOSEMITE NATIONAL PARK, CALIF.   J-264

El Capitan. Surely this is one of the most memorable features in the valley.

FISHERMAN'S PARADISE, YOSEMITE NATIONAL PARK, CALIF.   K-117

Fisherman's Paradise. This back-lit view of one of the many trout streams in Yosemite captures the beauty and appeal of the park. Those fortunate enough to drink their coffee in the brisk morning air won't soon forget the experience.

Le Conte Memorial Lodge. This lodge is named for Joseph Le Conte, a professor of geology, botany, and natural history, who died at Camp Curry on July 5, 1901. The lodge was built by the Sierra Club and was dedicated in 1904.

LE CONTE MEMORIAL LODGE, YOSEMITE NATIONAL PARK, CALIF. K-106

DEER IN THE GIANT FOREST, CALIF.   K-122

Deer in the Giant Forest. Wildlife abounds in the park and often appears tame and gentle. Park visitors should always remember that all animals in the park are wild. Bear and deer wander over the valley, wholly unafraid of man.

ARCH ROCK, ROAD TO YOSEMITE VALLEY, CALIF.   K-110

Arch Rock. This road still causes shrinking shoulders, ducking heads, and a few shrieks from unsuspecting tourists on a bus tour of the valley.

MOUNTAIN CABIN, YOSEMITE NATIONAL PARK, CALIF.   K-111

Mountain Cabin. Early residences like this are no longer part of the valley scene.

Lumber Camp in High Sierras. The lumber industry established itself early in and around the park. The Yosemite Grant preserved stands of timber within the parameters of the park, but the remains of sawmills and lumber camps are plentiful in the Sierras.

LUMBER CAMP IN HIGH SIERRAS. CALIF.   K-134

BRIDAL VEIL FALLS, YOSEMITE NATIONAL PARK. CALIF.   J-265

Bridalveil Fall. This beautiful fall frequently provides a romantic backdrop for couples.

UPPER AND LOWER YOSEMITE FALLS,

YOSEMITE NATIONAL PARK, CALIF.   J-266

Upper and Lower Yosemite Falls. The roar produced by the falls announces their presence long before the hiking tourist reaches the best view from the trail. On this card, Yosemite Falls drop like a long shining ribbon of white.

NEVADA FALLS FROM GLACIER POINT, YOSEM'TE NAT'L PARK, CALIF, K-106

Nevada Fall from Glacier Point. The most stupendous of all views is from Glacier Point, more than 3,250 feet straight above Camp Curry. From this vantage point, the distant snow-clad peaks are visible, and far below the Yosemite Valley appears as a miniature garden with both Nevada and Vernal Falls glistening in majestic beauty.

Bardell Fototone Miniatures, 20 Views of Yosemite (1922). The unknown photographer of this miniature print collection (each card is 3.5 by 2.25 inches) continued a long-standing tradition of photographing Yosemite. [FCL]

Yosemite Valley.

Yosemite Valley and Half Dome.

106

Inspiration Point. This magnificent park, for many years one of the most popular tourist attractions on the North American continent, where nature rises to unsurpassed heights of scenic grandeur, covers nearly 1,200 square miles (about the size of Rhode Island) on the western slope of the Sierra Nevada Mountains about 200 miles east of San Francisco.

Yosemite Valley. Yosemite has 429 lakes, a chain of mountain peaks averaging 10,000 feet, granite domes and monoliths, numerous trout streams, glaciers, and high meadows.

HALF DOME, YOSEMITE VALLEY, CAL.

Half Dome. Although only a small part of Yosemite National Park, Yosemite Valley with its bordering heights offers spectacular sights, such as Half Dome—4,892 feet, El Capitan—3,604 feet, and others—Three Brothers, Cathedral Spires, and Great North Dome.

EL CAPITAN, YOSEMITE VALLEY CAL.

El Capitan.

Glacier Point.

GLACIER POINT, YOSEMITE VALLEY, CAL.

THREE BROTHERS, YOSEMITE VALLEY, CAL.

Three Brothers.

109

EL CAPITAN AND THREE BROTHERS, YOSEMITE VALLEY, CALIF.

El Capitan and Three Brothers.

NORTH DOME, YOSEMITE VALLEY, CAL. Y/

North Dome.

110

Merced River.

Bridalveil, Yosemite, Vernal, and Nevada Falls. Some of the most awe-inspiring of all the scenery in the valley are the four great waterfalls, which drop from perpendicular cliffs high overhead from the valley floor.

Nevada Fall.

Camp Curry.

Mirror Lake. High above the Yosemite Valley lies a region of mountain peaks, swiftly rushing streams, and hundreds of lakes. Accessible during the summer season by means of trails for hikers and riders, fishermen and campers find it a true mountain paradise.

Yosemite Falls.

Vernal Fall.

Bridalveil Fall.

114

7764. Yosemite Valley from Artist Point, California.

Early Colored Souvenir Packet. This souvenir packet dates from c. 1915. It is unfortunately missing its front cover. It begins with Yosemite Valley from Artist Point. [GG17]

Cathedral Spires, Yosemite Valley, California.

Cathedral Spires.

Vernal Falls, Yosemite
Valley, California

Vernal Fall.

Three Brothers, Yosemite Valley, California.

Three Brothers.

Nevada Fall. Nevada Fall was named for its resemblance to an avalanche by the first white explorers in the valley. Nevada means "snow" in Spanish.

Mirror Lake. For a long while, Yosemite residents and park management fought against nature to retain Mirror Lake. An attempt was made by James Hutchings, an early innkeeper, to enlarge the lake area. Recent park management has determined to let nature take its course. The small lake is in the process of silting in and eventually will evolve into a water meadow—an open meadow encircled by trees—and finally a tree-covered spot.

117

Sierra Redwood Tree, the "Wawona." This is also known as the Tunnel Tree. Many tourists think there is only one tunnel tree in California, but in fact, there are several.

Half Dome, Yosemite Valley, California.

Half Dome.

Gates of Yosemite Valley.

Overhanging Rock, Glacier Point.

Fifteen Genuine Photographs by Sawyers This tourist's souvenir packet was printed for the Curry Company, c. 1921–22. Camp Curry was started by future concessionaires, David and Jennie Curry, in 1899. Seven tents on the site where Curry Village is today formed the genesis of a large commercial enterprise.

Real photograph packets were an aid to those who tried and failed to capture the classic views of Yosemite. From Carleton E. Watkins to Ansel Adams, hundreds of professional photographers have had a long-lasting love affair with Yosemite. [FCL]

Majestic View from Glacier Point.

The Wawona Tree. The 26-foot opening
was cut in August 1881.

Mirror Lake and Mt. Watkins.

Mirror Lake and Mt. Watkins - Yosemite Nat'l Park, Calif.

Arch Rock - Yosemite Nat'l Park

Arch Rock.

123

Sentinel Rock.

Half Dome.

Do NOT Feed the Bears. In the 1960s, park management ended a long-established tradition of feeding bears for the entertainment of tourists. Current policy treats and regards bears in Yosemite as wild animals not to be disturbed.

Gates of the Valley. North of the Tuolumne River is an enormous area of lakes and valleys not so frequently visited, although it is penetrated by numerous trails. The climax of the Sierra Nevada Mountains in this vicinity is reached at Mount Lyell (13,090 feet) on the eastern boundary of the park.

ACKNOWLEDGMENTS

We would like to thank Bill McCormick, the "postcard man," for making his entire collection of Yosemite postcards available to us. It took many years to accumulate such a collection, and Bill recognized the greater good when he relinquished his beloved postcards to the Fresno County Library, thereby making them accessible to the public and preserving them for historical purposes. We would also like to thank everyone in Fresno County who supported Measure B, the Public Library Tax Initiative in the 1999 local election. This book could not have been written without the funds that this tax has generated. Amazing how even one-eighth of one percent (.00125%) can make a difference. Support your local library!

We would like to acknowledge the corporate office of the Union Pacific Railroad in Omaha, Nebraska, for generously giving us permission to use a postcard for which they still hold copyright, at no charge.

The financial support of the Henry Madden Library at California State University, Fresno, should not be overlooked. It was this support that made the scanning of the postcards possible. That, as well as general support for the project as a whole, helped us along tremendously.

A big thank you to Allison Carpenter, our main contact person at Arcadia Publishing, and the one who patiently answered all of our questions, however asinine, outlandish, or tedious. Her cheerful helpfulness aided us throughout the project, especially during the painstaking layout process when we were pulling our hair out. Thanks for not giving up on us, Allison, and for listening to all of our crazy ideas.

Special thanks to Randy Vaughn-Dotta, photographer extraordinaire and master of his craft, whose help, expertise, and unflagging commitment to quality (not to mention his sense of humor, patience, and accommodating nature) made all the difference. Thanks, Randy. You're the best!

BIBLIOGRAPHY

Brower, Kenneth. *Yosemite: an American Treasure*. Washington, D.C.: National Geographic Society, 1990.

Darrah, William C. *The World of Stereographs*. Gettysburg, PA: W.C. Darrah, 1977.

Foley, D.J. *Foley's Yosemite Souvenir and Guide*, 7th ed. Yosemite, CA: Foley's Studio, [1905].

Gudde, Erwin, G. *California Place Names: a Geographical Dictionary*. Berkeley, CA: University of California Press, 1949.

Hartesveldt, Richard J. "Yosemite Valley Place Names," *Yosemite Nature Notes,* vol. XXXIV, no. 1 (1955): 1–22.

Hickman, Paul. *George Fiske, Yosemite Photographer*. Flagstaff, AZ: Northland Press, 1980.

Hutchings, James Mason. *Scenes of Wonder and Curiosity in California*. San Francisco: J.M. Hutchings & Co., 1862.

Johnson, Paul. *Yosemite*. Palo Alto, CA: Kodansha International, Ltd., 1970.

Johnston, Hank. *Railroads of the Yosemite Valley*. Glendale, CA: Trans-Anglo Books, 1963.

———. *The Yosemite Grant, 1864–1906: a Pictorial History*. Yosemite National Park: Yosemite Association, 1995.

———. *Yosemite's Yesterdays*. Yosemite, CA: Flying Spur Press, 1989.

Jones, William R. *Yosemite: the Story Behind the Scenery*. Las Vegas, NV: KC Publications, Inc., 1989.

Millar, June. "History of Fish Camp, Mariposa County." Unpublished manuscript, 1982.

Runte, Alfred. *Yosemite: the Embattled Wilderness*. Lincoln, NE: University of Nebraska Press, 1990.

Russell, Carl Parcher. *One Hundred Years in Yosemite: The Romantic Story of Early Human Affairs in the Central Sierra Nevada*. Palo Alto, CA: Stanford University Press, 1931.

Sanborn, Margaret. *Yosemite, its Discovery, its Wonders and its People*. New York: Random House, 1981.

Sargent, Shirley. *Enchanted Childhoods: Growing up in Yosemite, 1864–1945*. Yosemite, CA: Flying Spur Press, 1993.

———. *Pioneers in Petticoats, Yoesmite's Early Women, 1856–1900*. Los Angeles: Trans-Anglo Books, 1966.

———. *Yosemite and its Innkeepers, the Story of a Great Park and its Chief Concessionaires*. Yosemite, CA: Flying Spur Press, 1975.

Scharff, Robert, ed. *Yosemite National Park*. New York: David McKay Co., Inc., 1967.

Schlichtmann, Margaret. *The Big Oak Flat Road to Yosemite*. Fredericksburg, TX: Awani Press, 1986.

Woody, Howard. "International Postcards: Their History, Production and Distribution (Circa 1895 to 1915)." In *Delivering Views: Distant Cultures in Early Postcards*, Christraud M. Geary and Virginia-Lee Webb, eds. Washington, D.C.: Smithsonian Institution Press, 1998.

Yosemite: A Guide to Yosemite National Park, California. Washington, D.C.: U.S. Department of the Interior, 1990.

Yosemite National Park: A Word and Picture Journey through the World-Famous Yosemite National Park, with Thirty-One Full-Page Illustrations. Yosemite National Park: John Browne Jr., [1926?].

Yosemite: Saga of a Century. Oakhurst, CA: Sierra Star Press, 1964.